FAITH L...

Faith
An Important Subject To Man

47 facts you should know about the God-kind of faith

Akin Akintola

Unless otherwise indicated, all scripture quotations are taken from the King James Version of the Bible.

Faith An Important Subject To Man
ISBN 1 903284 00 7

Copyright © 1999 by Akin Akintola
Gospel Faith Ministries International
P.O.Box 802
Croydon CR9 8BB
United Kingdom
email: revakintola@hotmail.com

Published by **GFP Publishing**
P.O.Box 802
Croydon CR9 8BB
United Kingdom

Cover Design by *Him*Pressions — 020 7701 9919

Printed in the United Kingdom

All rights reserved under International Copyright Law. Contents and cover may not be reproduced in whole or in part in any form without express written permission of the publisher

CONTENTS

Acknowledgements
Dedication
Why I Wrote This Book! … 8

ORIGIN OF FAITH AND HOW IT COMES
FACT 1 — Faith Is In God's Word … 12
FACT 2 — Faith Comes By Hearing God, Consistently … 14

THE IMPORTANCE OF FAITH
FACT 3 — Only Through Faith Can Man Receive Salvation … 16
FACT 4 — What Is Not Of Faith Is Sin … 17

WHAT FAITH IS AND WHAT FAITH IS NOT
FACT 5 — Faith Is Not A Magical Word … 18
FACT 6 — Faith Is An Instruction From God … 20
FACT 7 — Faith Is The Raw Material Of Hope … 24
FACT 8 — Faith Is A Fact … 25
FACT 9 — Faith Is An Act … 25
FACT 10 — Faith Is A Catalyst … 26
FACT 11 — Faith Is A Gift … 27
FACT 12 — Faith Is A Fruit Of The Spirit … 28
FACT 13 — Faith Is A Shield … 29

FACT 14 —	Faith Is Always In The Now	30
FACT 15 —	Faith Is More Precious Than Gold	31
FACT 16 —	Faith Is An Overcoming Force	32

THE *MUST - BE'S* OF FAITH

FACT 17 —	Faith Must Be Developed	34
FACT 18 —	Faith Must Be In Your Heart And Mouth	35
FACT 19 —	Faith Must Be Preached	36

THE *CAN - BE'S* AND THE *CAN'S* OF FAITH

FACT 20 —	Faith Can Be Strong	39
FACT 21 —	Faith Can Be Rich	40
FACT 22 —	Faith Can Be Full	41
FACT 23 —	Faith Can Be Weak	42
FACT 24 —	Faith Can Be Little	44
FACT 25 —	Faith Can Be Unreal	45
FACT 26 —	Faith Can Be Stranded	46
FACT 27 —	Faith Can Be Perfect	47
FACT 28 —	Faith Can Be Great	47
FACT 29 —	Faith Can Be Seen	49
FACT 30 —	Faith Can Be Boosted By Prayer And Fasting	50
FACT 31 —	Faith Can Waiver	51
FACT 32 —	Faith Can Grow Exceedingly	54
FACT 33 —	Faith Can Make You Whole	54

THE *WILL'S* AND THE *WILL - BE'S* OF FAITH

FACT 34 —	Faith Will Attract An Enemy	56
FACT 35 —	Prayer Of Faith Will Heal The Sick	57
FACT 36 —	Prayer Of Faith Will Get God's Attention	58
FACT 37 —	Prayer Of Faith Will Produce Wisdom When Needed	59
FACT 38 —	Faith Will Be Tried ✓	59
FACT 39 —	Faith Will Be Made Impotent By Doubt, Unbelief And Fear	60
FACT 40 —	Faith Will Be Contend For	61
FACT 41 —	Faith will Be Spoken Of	62
FACT 42 —	Faith Will Be Built Up By Praying In The Will Of God	63

THE *SHOULD - BE* OF FAITH

FACT 43 —	Faith Should Be Motivated By Love	65

MORE FACTS ABOUT FAITH

FACT 44 —	Not Every Man Has Faith	67
FACT 45 —	Faith Is Given, In The Same Measure To Every Man	69
FACT 46 —	Faith Goes Only Where Hope Is ✓	70

THE ACCOMPLISHMENTS OF FAITH

FACT 47 —	Faith Has Accomplished Much	71

Dedication

This book is dedicated to...

My father; Akinbowale A. Akintola and my mother Janet O. Akintola who both dedicated me to the Lord and introduced me, my brothers and sisters to the Gospel of Christ. Thank you for this priceless heritage - may you both live long to reap all that you deserved.

To my son - Lawrence Akinbowale Akintola you have paid a great price in sharing your father with the demands of ministry and the challenges that comes with carrying the mantle of the anointing of Christ Jesus - thank you son! I love you very much.

And to the partners and friends of Gospel Faith Ministries International, your prayers and financial support as made this project a reality.

Acknowledgements

I thank God, my creator, my redeemer and my saviour - whom as called and chosen me to build His Kingdom and in Him I live, I move and I have my being.

To Pastor Agbo Oke -thank you for being there for me, your efforts in reading through the manuscripts and for taken off me some demands of ministry, to allow me time to finish this project.

To Pastor Ezekiel Ladapo - Your suggestions towards this book was very valuable. Thank you for reading through the manuscripts and for taken off me some ministry demands to allow me the time to finish this project.

To Pastor David Adesina - many thanks for your inputs and your stickability, all of these contributed to the realisation of this project.

To Mrs Jumoke Olumewo -I thank God for your life and having you as a sister both by birth and in Christ. Your time and inputs towards the making of this project a reality is very much appreciated.

May the good Lord continue to richly shower His blessings on you all!

Why I Wrote This Book!

Life itself is full of Storms and Adversities. Storms and Adversities are unavoidable part of Man's existence on Earth. But 'The Good God' has provided 'The Way' to overcome all, that life may throw at us.

This Way is Your Faith in God.

'... **And this is the victory that overcometh the world, even our faith.**'

1 John 5:4

God is the creator of Heaven and Earth and all that is contained in it.

'**For by Him were all things created, visible and invisible, whether they be thrones, or dominions, principalities, or powers: all things were created by Him, and for him.**'

Colossians 1:16

The God that created everything has stipulated the only way to please him.

'**But without faith it is impossible to please Him (God)...**' **(Italics added)**

Hebrews 11:6

And that is why Jesus said in Mark 11:22;

'... Have Faith in God.'

God has made his grace available to us all by the demonstration of his love in giving His only Son Jesus for the redemption of our sins;

> 'For all have sinned and fallen short of the Glory of God; being justified freely by his grace through the redemption that is in Christ Jesus:'
>
> **Romans 3:23-24**

> 'For God so loved the world, that he gave his only begotten Son, that whosoever believeth in him should not perish, but have everlasting life.'
>
> **John 3:16**

This grace is only, obtainable through Faith.

> 'For by grace are ye saved through faith; and not of yourselves: it is the gift of God: not of works, lest any man should boast.'
>
> **Ephesians 2:8**

God, through his grace has not planned any defeat or eternal damnation for man, but these blessings can only be appropriated by faith in God.

I am being fully persuaded that God, who is not a covenant breaker, will make good every one of His promises to man without fail.

'My covenant will I not break, nor alter the thing that is gone out of my lips. Once have I sworn by my holiness that I will not lie....'

Psalm 89:34-35

Having lived a life of faith in God, for over ten years now, I have developed an obsession for the word of God, which is his wisdom.

'Therefore also said the wisdom of God,'

Luke 11:49

'In the beginning was the Word, and the Word was with God, and the Word was God. And the Word was made flesh, and dwelt among us, (and we beheld his glory, the glory as of the only begotten of the father,) full of grace and truth.'

John 1:1,14

'Get wisdom, get understanding: forget it not; neither decline from the words of my mouth. Forsake her not, and she shall preserve thee: love her, and she shall keep thee. Wisdom is the principal thing; therefore get wisdom...'

Proverb 4:5-7

I have discovered 47 Powerful Biblical Facts about Faith, which I want you to know; to be assured of eternal life and to live in continuous overcoming, and fulfilling life in Christ Jesus.*'And wisdom and knowledge shall be the stability of thy times and strength of salvation: the fear of the LORD is his treasure.'* (Isaiah 33:6)

This is God's plan for you and that is what you will have, as you apply these facts to your life.

AKIN AKINTOLA

CHAPTER ONE

ORIGIN OF FAITH AND HOW IT WORKS

What is the origin of the God kind of Faith, you might ask? The answer is simple, "God". God is His word and this word is God. (John 1:1) His word is found in the Bible. The word also became flesh and dwelt among men. (John 1:14)

FACT 1

Faith Is In God's Word

God is His word. His word is found in the Bible. The word also became flesh and dwelt among men.

'In the beginning was the word, and the word was with God, and the word was God. And the word was made

flesh, and dwelt among us, (and we beheld his glory, the glory as of the only begotten of the father,) full of grace and truth.'

John 1:1&14

God is a Faith God and His word is full of Faith.

God created everything by his faith filled words.

'All things were made by him; and without him was not anything made that was made.'

John 1:3

God calleth things that be not as though they were.
Romans 4:17

God wanted man to hear his word, because Faith is in his word. So, by hearing His word faith will come.

'But what saith it? The word is nigh thee, even in thy mouth and in thy heart: that is, the word of faith, which we preach.' (Romans 10:8)

FAITH IS IN GOD'S WORD!

FACT 2

Faith Comes By Hearing God Consistently

Faith has to come, because faith was not there before.

'And that we may be delivered from unreasonable and wicked men: for all men have not faith.'

2 Thessalonians 3:2

Faith in God comes by hearing from God's mouth.

'...Man shall not live by bread alone, But by every word that proceedeth out of the mouth of God.'

Matthew 4:4

Faith comes by listening to God's inspired word when preached, taught in Church, on the radio, television, video or audiocassette and printed publications.*'So then faith cometh by hearing, and hearing by the Word of God'*(Romans 10:17).

FAITH COMES BY HEARING GOD CONSISTENTLY!

CHAPTER TWO

THE IMPORTANCE OF FAITH

The God kind of Faith is very important to man because, - the peaceful existence of man in the here and now - and beyond depends on it

"Therefore being justified by faith, we have peace with God through our Lord Jesus Christ".

Romans 5: 1

"For God so loved the world that He gave His only begotten Son, that whosoever believeth in him should not perish but have everlasting life. For God sent not His Son into the world to condemn the world; but the world through him might be saved. He that believeth on Him is not condemned; but he that believeth not is condemned already, because he hath not believed in the name of the only begotten Son of God."

John 3:16-18

FAITH AN IMPORTANT SUBJECT TO MAN

FACT 3

Only Through Faith Can Man Receive Salvation

Faith is the most important subject to man.

For without faith, man cannot please God.

Also without faith, man cannot receive God's gift of salvation from sin and it's consequences.

' For all have sinned, and come short of the glory of God; being justified freely by grace through the redemption that is in Christ Jesus.'

Romans 3:23-24

'For by grace are ye saved through faith; and that not of yourselves...'

Ephesians 2:8

THE FORGIVENESS OF SIN ONLY COMES THROUGH FAITH IN CHRIST JESUS THE SON OF GOD!

FACT 4

What Is Not Of Faith Is Sin

God is a Faith God. He created man in his Image and after His likeness. (Genesis 1:27)

God wanted man to have faith in him, to talk like He talks and walk like He walks.

God calls things that be not, as though they were.

> **' ... And calleth those things which be not as though they were.'**
>
> **Romans 4:17**

God talks faith and so every one that, He created should talk faith like God.

This is why he wanted man to hear from him, so faith can come. Failure to hear from God means that Faith will not come to you, and you will not talk and live by Faith.

> **' ... for whatsoever is not of faith is sin.'**
>
> **Romans 14:23**

WHAT IS NOT OF FAITH IS SIN!

CHAPTER THREE

WHAT FAITH IS AND WHAT FAITH IS NOT

What Faith is - can best be comprehended by understanding what faith is not.

FACT 5

Faith Is Not A Magic Word

When faith comes to a man, it triggers a series of processes - which I call 'The Faith Cycle', because God works in cycles and everything in life goes through cycles.

Faith will always attract trials, in 1 Peter 1:7; Apostle Peter wrote by the inspiration of The Holy Spirit; that faith will be tried. *'The trying of your faith,….'*

Also in James 1: 3-4 it is mentioned that faith will be tried and the trial of faith worketh patience.

'Knowing this, that the trying of your faith worketh patience. But let patience have her perfect work, that you may be perfect and entire, wanting nothing.'

In the epistle to the Romans chapter 5: 3-5 we see the other forces that faith directly and indirectly puts to work.

'And not only so, but we glory in tribulations also; knowing that tribulations worketh patience; And patience, experience; and experience, hope: And hope maketh not ashamed;....'

FAITH CYCLE

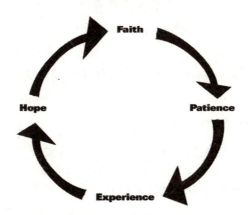

FAITH IS NOT A MAGIC WORD - BUT TRIGGERS A SERIES OF PROCESSES.

FACT 6

Faith Is An Instruction From God

'...but by the law of faith.'

Romans 3:27

Faith is not a suggestion, neither is it a good idea, but a strong instruction from God to man, in order that man can benefit from His Plans. In five different passages in the Bible; the Just (those in right standing with God) are instructed to live by faith.

'... but the just shall live by faith.'

Habakkuk 2:4

'... As it is written, The just shall live by faith.'

Romans 1:17

'For we walk by faith, not by sight:'

2 Corinthians 5:7

'Now the just shall live by faith: but if any man draw back, my soul shall have no pleasure in him.'

Hebrews 10:38

'But that no man is justified by the law in the sight of God, it is evident: for, The just shall live by faith.'

Galatians 3:11

The heavens and the earth were created by God's faith filled words.

'In the beginning God created the heaven and the earth. And the earth was without form, and void; and darkness was upon the face of the deep. And the Spirit of God moved upon the face of the waters.

'And God said, let there be light: and there was light. And God saw the light, that it was good: and God divided the light from the darkness. And God called the light Day, and the darkness he called Night. And the evening and the morning were the first day.

'And God said, let there be a firmament in the midst of the waters.

And God made the firmament, and divided the waters which were under the firmament from the waters which were above the firmament: and it was so.

And God called the firmament Heaven. And the evening and the morning were the second day.

'And God said, Let the waters under the heaven be gathered together unto one place, and let the dry land appear: and it was so.

And God called the dry land Earth; and the gathering together of the waters called he seas: and God saw that it was good.

'And God said, Let the earth bring forth grass, the herb yielding seed, and the fruit tree yielding fruit after his kind, whose seed is in itself, upon the earth: and it was so.

And the earth brought forth grass, and herb yielding seed after his kind, and the tree yielding fruit, whose

FAITH AN IMPORTANT SUBJECT TO MAN

seed was in itself, after his kind: and God saw that it was good. And the evening and the morning were the third day.

'And God said, let there be lights in the firmament of the heaven to divide the day from the night; and let them be for signs, and for seasons, and for days and years:

'And let them be for lights in the firmament of the heaven to give light upon the earth: and it was so.

And God made two great lights; the greater light to rule the day, and the lesser light to rule the night: he made the stars also.

'And God set them in the firmament of the heaven to give light upon the earth, And to rule over the day and over the night, and to divide the light from the darkness: and God saw that it was good.

And the evening and the morning were the fourth day.

'And God said, let the waters bring forth abundantly the moving creature that hath life, and fowl that may fly above the earth in the open firmament of heaven. And God created great whales, and every living creature that moveth, which the waters brought forth abundantly, after their kind, and every winged fowl after his kind: and God saw that it was good.

'And God blessed them saying, be fruitful, and multiply, and fill the waters in the seas, and let fowl multiply in the earth. And the evening and the morning were the fifth day. 'And God said, Let the earth bring forth the living creature after his kind, cattle, and creeping thing, and beast of the earth after his kind: and it was so.

And God made the beast of the earth after his kind, and cattle after their kind, and every thing that creepeth upon the earth after his kind: and God saw that it was good.

What Faith Is And What Faith Is Not

> 'And God said, Let us make man in our image, after our likeness: and let them have dominion over the fish of the sea, and over the fowl of the air, and over the cattle, and over all the earth, and over every creeping thing that creepeth upon the earth. 'So God created man in his own image, in the image of God created he him; male and female created he them.
>
> 'And God Blessed them, and God said unto them, Be fruitful, and multiply, and replenish the earth, and subdue it: and have dominion over the fish of the sea, and over the fowl of the air, and over every living thing that moveth upon the earth. 'And God said, Behold, I have given you every herb bearing seed, which is upon the face of all the earth, and every tree, in the which is the fruit of a tree yielding seed; to you it shall be for meat.
>
> And to every beast of the air, and to every thing that creepeth upon the earth, wherein there is life, I have given every green herb for meat: and it was so.'
>
> **Genesis 1:1-30**

To partake in any of God's Plan for man, you need faith. Even God's redemptive plan for man can only be obtained by faith.

> 'For by grace are ye saved through faith; and not of yourselves: it is the gift of God: not of works, least any man should boast.'
>
> **Ephesians 2:8-9**

FAITH IS A INSTRUCTION FROM GOD AND ONLY BY FAITH CAN MAN PLEASE GOD!

FAITH AN IMPORTANT SUBJECT TO MAN

FACT 7

Faith Is The Raw Material Of Hope

'Now faith is the substance of things hoped for,'

Hebrew 11:1

Man's hope in God, need's the ingredient of faith to transform what is hoped for, to a reality.

Just as a farmer needs the raw material of seeds to sow, before he can expect to reap the harvest of the seeds sown, - likewise man needs faith.

Faith is the ingredient required in reaping God's blessings.

FAITH IS THE RAW MATERIAL OF HOPE!

FACT 8

Faith Is A Fact

'... the evidence of things not seen.'

Hebrew 11:1

Faith is a proof.

Faith is Tangible.

Faith take's hold of God's promises.

Faith is the confirmation and conviction of things we are yet to see.

FAITH IS A FACT!

FACT 9

Faith Is An Act

Faith without corresponding action is dead.

'What doth it profit; my brethren, though a man say, he hath faith, and have not works? can faith save him? If a brother or sister be naked, and destitute of daily food, And one of you say unto them, Depart in peace, be ye

FAITH AN IMPORTANT SUBJECT TO MAN

warmed and filled; not withstanding ye give them not those things which are needful to the body; what doth it profit?

Even so faith, if it hath not works, is dead, being alone. Yea, a man may say, Thou has faith, and I have works: shew me thy faith without thy works and I will shew thee my faith by my works.

Thou believest that there is one God; thou doest well; the devils also believe, and tremble. But wilt thou know, o vein man, that faith without works is dead?

James 2: 14- 20

THEREFORE, FAITH IS AN ACT!

FACT 10

Faith Is A Catalyst

A catalyst is a substance that aids, speeds-up or triggers a process in which itself, does not under-go any changes. (Oxford Advanced Learners Dictionary)

Faith attracts trials and tribulations in the life of a man who has connected to faith, the tribulations and trials worketh patience and patience worketh experience and experience worketh hope.

And faith substance remained unchanged in the entire process.

> 'Knowing this, that the trying of your faith worketh patience. But let patience have her perfect work, that ye may be perfect and entire, wanting nothing.'
>
> **James 1:3-4**

In Romans 5:3-5; we see the catalystic effect of faith *'… but we glory in tribulations also; knowing that tribulation worketh patience; And patience, experience; and experience, hope: And hope maketh not ashamed….'*

FAITH IS A CATALYST!

FACT 11

Faith Is A Gift

A gift is a demonstration of Love.

Faith is a gift given to man by God through the Holy Spirit.

> 'For God so Loved the world, that He gave His only begotten Son,…'
>
> **John 3: 16**

The Holy Spirit is the giver of faith.

FAITH AN IMPORTANT SUBJECT TO MAN

'Now there are diversities of gifts, but the same Spirit. And there are differences of administrations, but the same Lord.

And there are diversities of operations, but it is the same God, which worketh all in all. But the manifestation of the Spirit is given to every man to profit withal.

For to one is given by the Spirit the word of wisdom; to another the word of knowledge by the same Spirit:

To another Faith by the same Spirit; ...'

1 Corinthians 12:4-9

FAITH IS A GIFT!

FACT 12

Faith Is A Fruit of the Spirit

An Apple is a fruit of the Apple tree.

An Orange is a fruit of the Orange tree.

Faith is a fruit of the Holy Spirit; which means faith is a fruit that comes from the Holy Spirit.

'But the fruit of the Spirit is Love, joy, peace, longsuffering, gentleness, goodness, faith, Meekness, temperance:...'

Galatians 5:22-23

FAITH IS A FRUIT OF THE SPIRIT!

FACT 13

Faith Is A Shield

The believer in Christ Jesus needs the shield of faith in conjunction with the other weapons of God at the disposal of the believer, in order to withstand in the day of trouble, and when the trouble is over to adhere to the profession of faith.

> 'Wherefore take unto you the whole armour of God, that ye may be able to withstand in the evil day, and having done all, to stand.
>
> Stand therefore, having your loins girt about with truth, and having on the breastplate of righteousness; And your feet shod with the preparation of the gospel of peace; Above all, taking the shield of faith wherewith ye shall be able to quench all the fiery darts of the wicked. And take the helmet of salvation, and the sword of the Spirit, which is the Word of God: Praying always with all prayer and supplication in the Spirit, and watching there unto with all perseverance...'
>
> **Ephesians 6:13-18**

(For Further insight into the believers Weapon, Listen to my 5 Tape Audio Series Titled 'Call to War')

FAITH AN IMPORTANT SUBJECT TO MAN

The shield of faith when used will enable the believer to intercept the arrows from the evil-one and make it of no effect.

FAITH IS A SHIELD!

FACT 14

Faith Is Always In The Now

'Now, faith is...'

Hebrew 11:1

Faith is never in the future. Faith is always NOW!

'Now the Just shall live by faith: but if any man draw back, my soul shall have no pleasure in him.' (Hebrews 10:38)

'But without faith it is impossible to please him: for he that cometh to God must believe that he is...'

Hebrews 11:6

'For verily I say unto you, that whosoever shall say unto this mountain, Be thou removed, and be thou cast into the sea; and shall not doubt in his heart, but shall believe that those things which he saith shall come to pass; he shall have whatsoever he saith.

What Faith Is And What Faith Is Not

Therefore I say unto you, what things soever ye desire, when ye pray, believe (have Faith) (Italics added) that ye receive them, and ye shall have them.'

Mark 11:23-24

FAITH IS ALWAYS IN THE NOW!

FACT 15

Faith Is More Precious Than Gold

'That the trial of your faith, being much more precious than of gold that perisheth, though it be tried with fire, might be found unto praise and honor and glory at the appearing of Jesus Christ: who having not seen, ye love; in whom, though now ye see him not, yet believing, ye rejoice with joy, yet believing, ye rejoice with joy unspeakable and full of glory: receiving the end of your faith, even the salvation of your souls.'

1 Peter 1:7-9

FAITH IS MORE VALUABLE THAN GOLD!

FAITH AN IMPORTANT SUBJECT TO MAN

FACT 16

Faith Is An Overcoming Force

'For whatsoever is born of God overcometh the world: and this is the victory that overcometh the world, even our faith. Who is he that overcometh the world, but he that believeth that Jesus is the son of God? This is he that came by water and blood, even Jesus Christ; not by water only, but by water and blood. And it is the Spirit that beareth witness, because the Spirit is truth.' (1 John 5:4-6).

FAITH IS AN OVERCOMING FORCE

CHAPTER FOUR

THE *MUST — BE'S* OF FAITH

When Faith comes to a man, there are certain things which must be done to it, in order for it to be what it should be, to the person that faith has come to. These things are what I have called the Must — Be's of Faith.

Just as in the natural, when a baby is born - there are things that must be done to the baby - for that baby to grow-up into a healthy and responsible-adulthood. Likewise the God kind of faith has things which must be done to it. The following are the Must — Be's of Faith.

FACT 17

Faith Must Be Developed

Every child of God, has been given the same measure of faith. (Romans 12:3) You can not have any more faith than you have been given already, but you can develop what you have been given, to become stronger.

It takes only a strong faith to birth the blessings of God in the midst of conflicting situations.

> 'And being not weak in faith, he considered not his own body now dead, when he was about an hundred years old, neither yet the deadness of Sarah's womb: He staggered not at the promise of God through unbelief; but was strong in faith, giving glory to God.'
>
> **Romans 4: 19-20**

By doing the following, faith can be developed:

1. Feed yourself on the Word of God.

'... *Man shall not live by bread alone, But by every word that proceedeth out of the mouth of God*' (Matthew 4:4).

2. Exercise your faith by using it.

Faith without corresponding action is dead.

'Even so faith, if it hath not works, is dead, being alone. But wilt thou know O vain man, that faith without works is dead? Seest thou how faith wrought with his works, and by works was faith made perfect?' (James 2:17,20 & 22).

'Now the Just shall live by faith,'(Hebrew 10:38).

FAITH MUST BE DEVELOPED!

FACT 18

Faith Must Be In Your Heart And Mouth

God told Joshua that His word must be in his mouth all the time. And that he must meditate on His word consistently until he possesses the Promised Land.

> **'This book of the Law shall not depart out of thy mouth: but thou shalt meditate therein day and night, that thou mayest observe to do according to all that is written therein: for then thou shall make thy way prosperous, and then thou shalt have good success.'**
>
> **Joshua 1:8**

FAITH AN IMPORTANT SUBJECT TO MAN

Proverb 4:21; says

'Let them not depart from thine eyes; keep them in the midst of thine heart.'

And verse 24; says

'Put away from thee a froward mouth, and perverse lips put far from thee.'

The word of faith must be in your heart and mouth, to be potent and effective.

'That if thou shall confess with thy mouth the Lord Jesus, and shalt believe in thine heart, that God hath raised him from the dead, thou shalt be saved. For with the heart man believeth unto righteousness; and with the mouth confession is made unto salvation.'

Romans 10: 9-10

FAITH MUST BE IN YOUR HEART AND MOUTH!

FACT 19

Faith Must Be Preached

Man needs to hear the word of Faith (God's Word). So, man can have faith, because faith comes only by hearing from God.

'... That is the word of faith which we preach:'

Romans 10:8

God wants man to have faith.

> 'And Jesus answering saith unto them, Have faith in God.'
>
> **Mark 11:22**

But faith can only be heard when it is preached or proclaimed.

> 'How then shall they call on him in whom they have not believed? And how shall they believe in him of whom they have not heard? And how shall they hear without a preacher?'
>
> **Romans 10:14**

FAITH MUST BE PREACHED!

CHAPTER FIVE

THE *CAN - BE'S* AND THE *CAN'S* OF FAITH

Faith has potentialities and faith can also perform less than its optimum performance from time to time - depending on how it has been nourished and developed. These potentialities are what I called The Can — Be's and the Can's of Faith.

Just as a baby has the potential to grow into a responsible, strong, healthy adulthood and into old age. The opposite can also be true - if that baby is not well nourished and groomed. This also can happen to faith. The following are The Can — Be's and the Can's of Faith.

FACT 20

Faith Can Be Strong

God wants us to have a strong faith.

'And Jesus answering saith unto them, Have faith in God. For verily I say unto you, that whosoever shall say unto this mountain, Be thou removed, and be thou cast into the sea; and shall not doubt in his heart, but shall believe that those things which he saith shall come to pass; he shall have whatsoever he saith.

Mark 11: 22-23

Abraham, the father of faith had a strong faith that is how he became the father of many nations.

'He staggered not at the promises of God through unbelief, but was strong in faith, giving glory to God.'

Romans 4:20

Your faith can be made strong by the following:

1. Your faith can remain strong in the midst of adversity by fixing your focus on God's promises through his word. *'Looking on to Jesus the author and finisher of our faith; who for the joy that was set before him endured the cross, despising the shame, and is set down at the right hand of the throne of God'* (Hebrew 12:2).

FAITH AN IMPORTANT SUBJECT TO MAN

2. Maintaining a strong praise life *'...but was strong in faith. Giving glory to God'* (Romans 4:20).

3. Put on the whole amour of God. *'Be strong in the Lord, and in the power of his might. Put on the whole armour of God, that ye may be able to stand against the wiles of the devil'* (Ephesians 6:10-11).

FAITH CAN BE STRONG!

FACT 21

Faith Can Be Rich

Richness suggests having more than enough for the present need; and enough for the future need.

You can have more than enough faith to overcome any adversity in life.

When your faith is rich, it means you have more than you need presently, and you also have enough now to meet your future need.

In James 2:5; the Bible says:

'Hearken, my beloved brethren, Hath not God chosen the poor of this world rich in faith, and heirs of the kingdom which he hath promised to them that love him?'

God wants us to be rich in faith.

SO, FAITH CAN BE RICH!

FACT 22

Faith Can Be Full

You can be full of faith, that is: you have faith in your heart, mouth and you have works to back it up.

In the book of Acts 6:8 the account of Stephen a deacon, in the early church, a man full of faith, whose heart is focused right, his talk is right and his walk is consistent with his faith profession.

> **'And Stephen, full of faith and power, did great wonders and miracles among the people.**

Barnabas was also mentioned in Acts 11:24 as a man full of faith.

> **'... and they send forth Barnabas that he should go as far as Antioch. Who when he came, and has seen the grace of God, was glad, and exhorted them all, that with purpose of heart they would cleave unto the Lord. For he was a good man and full of the Holy Ghost and of faith: and much people was added unto the Lord. Then departed Barnabas to Tarsus, for to seek Saul: And when he had found him, he brought him unto Antioch. And it came to pass, that a whole year they assembled themselves with the church, and taught much people. And the disciples were called Christians first in Antioch.**
>
> **Acts 11:23-26**

FAITH CAN BE FULL!

FAITH AN IMPORTANT SUBJECT TO MAN

FACT 23

Faith Can Be Weak

Faith can be weak. So, you don't assume that your faith is going to stay strong without you keeping it strong.

Abraham the 'father of faith ' did not instantly became strong in faith. In fact, Abraham initially found it hard to believe what God has said would come to pass in his life and in the life of Sarah his wife.

> 'And God said unto Abraham, As for Sarai thy wife, thou shalt not call her name Sarai, but Sarah shall her name be. And I will bless her, and give thee a son also of her: yea, I will bless her, and she shall be a mother of nations; king of people shall be of her. Then Abraham fell upon his face, and laughed, and said in his heart, shall a child be born unto him that is an hundred years old? And shall Sarah, that is ninety years old, bear?'
>
> **Genesis 17:15-17**

> 'And they said unto him where is Sarah thy wife? And he said, Behold, in the tent. And he said I will certainly return unto thee according to the time of life; and, lo, Sarah thy wife shall have a son. And Sarah heard it in the tent door, which was behind him. Now Abraham and Sarah were old and well stricken in age; and it ceased to

> be with Sarah after the manner of women. Therefore Sarah laughed with herself, saying, After I, am waxed old shall I have pleasure, my lord being old also? And the Lord said unto Abraham, wherefore did Sarah laugh, saying, shall I of a surety bear a child, which am old?'
>
> **Genesis 18:9-13**

Now you see, that your faith is not going to be automatically strong, you will have to build up from its weak state to being strong. Abraham and Sarah had to build their faith up strong, before they experienced God's promise in their lives.

> 'As it is written, I have made thee a father of many nations, before him whom he believed, even God, who quickeneth the dead, and calleth those things which be not as though they were. Who against hope believed in hope, that he might become the father of many nations, according to that which was spoken, so shall thy seed be. And being not weak in faith, he considered not his own body now dead, when he was about an hundred years old, neither yet the deadness of Sarah's womb: He staggered not at the promise of God through unbelief; but was strong in faith, giving glory to God; And being fully persuaded, that what he had promised, he was able also to perform. And therefore it was imputed to him for righteousness.
>
> **Romans 4:17-22**

FAITH CAN BE WEAK!

FAITH AN IMPORTANT SUBJECT TO MAN

FACT 24

Faith Can Be Little

Faith can be little; in Matthew chapter 14:25-31;

'And in the fourth watch of the night Jesus went unto them, walking on the sea. And when the disciples saw him walking on the sea, they were troubled, saying it is a spirit, and they cried out for fear. But straightway Jesus spake unto them, saying, be of good cheer; it is I; be not afraid. And Peter answered him and said, Lord, If it be thou, bid me come unto thee on the water. And he said, come. And when Peter was come down out of the ship, he walked on the water, to go to Jesus. But when he saw the wind boisterous, he was afraid; and beginning to sink, he cried, saying Lord, save me. And immediately Jesus stretched forth his hand, and caught him, and said unto him, O thou of little faith, wherefore didst thou doubt?

The word 'little' in the Greek means: Lacking in confidence according to 'The Strong's Exhaustive Concordance of the Bible'. Which means that verse 31 of Matthew 14: should read like this: '… you are lacking in faith, why did you doubt?

In Matthew 6:24-26:

'… there arose a great tempest in the sea, insomuch that the ship was covered with the waves: but he was asleep. And his disciples came to him, and awoke him, saying,

> Lord, save us: we perish. And he said unto them, why are ye so fearful, o ye of little faith? Then he arose, and rebuked the winds and the sea; and there was a great calm.'

Also in Matthew 16:8

> '... Jesus perceived, he said unto them, o ye of little faith, why reason ye among yourselves, because ye have brought no bread?

God did not want our faith little or lacking, but to remain strong always as we maintain a strong prayer and praise life, which will help us keep our focus fixed on God's promises.

FAITH CAN BE LITTLE!

FACT 25

Faith Can Be Unreal

Faith can be real, so also, faith can be unreal.

A real faith, will talk the talk, and will walk the walk.

> 'Neither give heed to fables and endless genealogies, which minister questions, rather than godly edifying which is in faith: so do. Now the end of the commandment is charity out of a pure heart, and of a good conscience, and

of Faith unfeigned: From which some having swerved have turned aside unto vain jangling.'

1Timothy 1:4-6

FAITH CAN BE UNREAL!

FACT 26

Faith Can Be Stranded

A stranded faith is a shipwrecked faith. A Faith that did not deliver what it should deliver. A man that focuses on adverse circumstances, and not on the promises and the faithfulness of God will suffer a shipwreck faith.

> 'This charge I commit unto thee, son Timothy, according to the prophecies which went before on thee, that thou by them mightest war a good warfare: holding faith, and a good conscience; which some having put away, concerning faith have made shipwreck:'

1 Timothy 1:18-19

Peter's faith was shipwrecked when he took his eyes off Jesus and looked at the boisterous wind.

> 'But when he saw the wind boisterous, he was afraid; and beginning to sink, he cried, saying Lord, save me.'

Matthew 14:30

FAITH CAN BE STRANDED!

FACT 27

Faith Can Be Perfect

'But wilt thou know, o vain man, that faith without works is dead?

Was not Abraham our father justified by works, when he had offered Isaac his son upon the altar?

Seest thou how faith wrought with works, and by works was faith made perfect?

James 2:20-22

Faith can be perfect, that means it's complete, and will accomplish anything in God, that it is applied to, with the corresponding actions.

FAITH CAN BE PERFECT!

FACT 28

Faith Can Be Great

'The centurion answered and said, Lord, I am not worthy that thou shouldest come under my roof: but speak the word only, and my servant shall be healed. For I am a man under authority, having soldiers under me and I say

FAITH AN IMPORTANT SUBJECT TO MAN

this man, Go, and he goeth; and to another, come, and he cometh; and to my servant, do this, and he doeth it. When Jesus heard it, he marveled, and said to them that followed, verily I say unto you, I have not found so great faith, no, not in Israel. And Jesus said unto the centurion, Go thy way; and as thou hast believed, so be it done unto thee. And his servant was healed in the selfsame hour.

Matthew 8:8-10 & 13

'And, behold, a woman of Canaan came out of the same coasts, and cried unto him, saying, Have mercy on me, o Lord, thou son of David; my daughter is grievously vexed with a devil. But he answered her not a word. And his disciples came and besought him, saying, send her away; for she crieth after us. But he answered and said, I am not sent but unto the lost sheep of the house of Israel. Then came she and worshipped him, saying, Lord, help me. But he answered and said, it is not meet to take the children's bread, and to cast it to dogs. And she said, Truth, Lord: yet the dogs eat of the crumbs, which fall from their masters' table. Then Jesus answered and said unto her, o woman, great is thy faith: be it unto thee even as thou wilt. And her daughter was made whole from that very hour.

Matthew 15:22-28

Faith can be great, which means that faith can standout - make an impression or worthy.

YOUR FAITH CAN STANDOUT!

FACT 29

Faith Can Be Seen

'And, behold, men brought in a bed a man, which was taken with a palsy: and they sought means to bring him in, and to lay him before him. And when they could not find by what way they might bring him in because of the multitude, they went upon the housetop, and let him down through the tiling with his couch into the midst before Jesus. And when Jesus saw their faith, He said unto him, man, thy sins are   forgiven thee.'

Luke 5:18-20

'And behold, they brought to him a man sick of palsy, lying on a bed: And Jesus seeing their faith said unto the sick of the palsy; so, be of good cheer; thy sins be forgiven thee.'

Matthew 9:2

Faith can be seen through the corresponding actions of faith that we take!

FAITH CAN BE SEEN!

FAITH AN IMPORTANT SUBJECT TO MAN

FACT 30

Faith Can Be Boosted By Prayer And Fasting

'And when they come to the multitude, there came to him a certain man, kneeling down to him, and saying, Lord, have mercy on my son; for he is lunatic, and sore vexed: for oftentimes he falleth into the fire, and often into water. And I brought him to thy disciples, and they could not cure him.

Then Jesus answered and said, o faithless and perverse generation, how long shall I be with you? How long shall I suffer you? Bring him hither to me. And Jesus rebuked the devil; and he departed out of him: and the child was cured from that very hour.

Then came the disciples to Jesus apart, and said, why could not we cast him out? And Jesus said unto them, because of your unbelief: for verily I say unto you, if ye have faith as a grain of mustard seed, ye shall say unto this mountain, remove hence to yonder place; and it shall remove: and nothing shall be impossible unto you.

Howbeit this kind goeth not out but by prayer and fasting.

Matthew 17:14-21

'This kind can come forth by nothing, but by Prayer and Fasting.'

Mark 9:29

FAITH CAN BE BOOSTED BY PRAYER AND FASTING!

FACT 31

Faith Can Waiver

'But let him ask in faith, nothing wavering. for he that wavereth is like a wave of the sea driven with the wind and tossed. for let not that man think that he shall receive any thing of the Lord.'

James 1:6-7

Faith can waiver, but God did not want our faith to waiver. He wants our faith to stand strong, even in the midst of storms.

Faith Will Waiver When We Do The Following:

1. Focus On the Circumstances.

'... He considered not his own body now dead, when he was about an hundred years old, neither yet the deadness of Sarah's womb' (Romans 4:19).

2. Given In To Our Feelings.

'Who against hope believed in hope, that he might become the father of many nations, according to that

FAITH AN IMPORTANT SUBJECT TO MAN

which was spoken, so shall thy seed be' (Romans 4:18).

3. Relying On Own Interpretation of What We see and hear.

'And a woman having an issue of blood twelve years, which had spent all her living upon physicians, neither could be healed of any. Came behind him, and touched the boarder of his garment: and immediately her issue of blood stanched' (Luke 8:43-44).

4. Relying On What Others Say about Our Situation.

'And behold, there came a man named Jairus, and he was a ruler of the synagogue: and he fell down at Jesus feet, and be sought him that he would come into his house: For he had one only daughter, about twelve years of age, and she lay a dying ... While he yet spake, there cometh one from the ruler of the Synagogue's house, saying to him, thy daughter is dead; trouble not the master. But when Jesus heard it, he answered him, saying, fear not believe only, and she shall be made whole. And when he came into the house, he suffered no man to go in, save Peter and James, and John, and the father and the mother of the maiden. And all wept, and bewailed her: but he said, weep not; she is not dead, but sleepeth. And they laughed him to scorn, knowing that she was dead. And he put them all out, and took her by the hand, and called, saying, maid, arise. And her spirit came again, and she arose straightway: and he commanded to give her meat' (Luke 8:41-55).

5. Listening To the Lies of the Adversary.

'And they said one to another, Behold, this dreamer cometh. Come now therefore, and we will say, some evil beast hath devoured him: and we shall see what will become of his dreams' (Genesis 37:19-20).

'But the Lord was with Joseph, and shewed him mercy, and gave him favour in the sight of the keeper of the prison. The keeper of the prison looked not to any thing that was under his hand; because the Lord was with him, and that which he did, the Lord made it to prosper' (Genesis 39:21 & 23).

'Then Pharaoh sent and called Joseph and they brought him hastily out of the dungeon: and he shaved himself, and changed his raiment, and came in unto Pharaoh. And Pharaoh said unto Joseph, Forasmuch as God hath shewed thee all this, there is none so discreet and wise as thou art: Thou shalt be over my house, and according unto thy word shall all my people be ruled: only in the throne will I be greater than thou will. And Pharaoh said unto Joseph, see, I have set thee over all the land of Egypt' (Genesis 41:14,39-41).

FAITH CAN WAIVER, BUT YOU MUST KEEP IT STRONG THROUGHOUT!

FACT 32

Faith Can Grow Exceedingly

'We are bound to thank God always for you, brethren, as it is meet, because that your faith groweth exceedingly, and the charity of every one of you all toward each other aboundeth;'

2 Thessalonians 1:3

'And the grace of our Lord was exceeding abundant with faith and love which is in Christ Jesus.'

Timothy 1:14

Faith can grow more and more.
FAITH CAN GROW EXCEEDINGLY!

FACT 33

Faith Can Make You Whole

The word whole can be described as the state of completeness and restoration — *nothing missing, nothing broken.*

Jesus told the woman with the issue of blood, that her faith has made her whole.

> 'But the woman fearing and trembling. Knowing what was done in her, came and fell down before him, and told him all the truth. And he said unto her, Daughter, thy faith hath made thee whole; go in peace, and be whole of thy plague.'
>
> **Mark 5:33-34**

In Mark 10:52;

> 'Jesus said unto him, go thy way; thy faith hath made thee whole. And immediately he received his sight, and followed Jesus in the way.'

Also in Luke 17:12-19

> 'And as he entered into a certain village, there met him ten men that were lepers, which stood a far off: And they lifted up their voices, and said, Jesus, master, have mercy on us. And when he saw them, he said unto them, go shew yourselves unto the priests. And it came to pass that as they went they were cleansed. And one of them, when he saw that he was healed, turned back, and with a loud voice glorified God, And fell down on his face at his feet, giving him thanks: and he was a Samaritan. And Jesus answering said, was there not ten cleansed? But where are the nine? There are not found that returned to give glory to God, save this stranger. And he said unto him, arise, go thy way: thy faith hath made thee whole.'

FAITH CAN MAKE YOU WHOLE!

CHAPTER SIX

THE *WILL'S* AND THE *WILL - BE'S* OF FAITH

The God kind of faith, has causes and effects - which I called The Will's and The Will — Be's of faith, which are as follows:

FACT 34

Faith Will Attract An Enemy

'And Stephen, full of faith and power, did great wonders and miracles among the people. Then there arose certain of the Synagogue, which is called the Synagogue of the Libertines, and Cyrenians, and Alexandrians, and of them of Cilicia and of Asia, disputing with Stephen. And they were not able to resist the wisdom and the Spirit by which he spake. Then they suborned men, which said, we have heard him speak blasphemous words against Moses, and against God. And they stirred up the people, and the elders, and the scribes, and came upon him, and caught him, and brought him to the council. And set up false witness, which said, this man ceaseth not to speak blaphemous words against this holy place, and the law: For we have heard him say, that this Jesus of Nazareth shall destroy this place, and shall change the customs which Moses delivered us.'

Acts 6:8-14

FAITH WILL ATTRACT AN ENEMY!

FACT 35

Prayer Of Faith Will Heal The Sick

'*Is any sick among you? Let him call for the elders of the church; and let them pray over him, anointing him with oil in the name of the Lord: And the prayer of faith shall save the sick...*' (James 5:14-15).

THE PRAYER OF FAITH WILL HEAL THE SICK

FAITH AN IMPORTANT SUBJECT TO MAN

FACT 36

Prayer Of Faith Will Get God's Attention

'Let us therefore come boldly unto the throne of grace, that we may obtain mercy, and find grace to help in time of need' (Hebrews 4:16).

'And this is the confidence we have in him, that if we ask anything according to his will, he heareth us: And if we know that he hears us, whatsoever we ask, we know that we have the petitions that we desire of him.' (1 John 14-15)

'Therefore I say unto, what things soever ye desire, when ye pray, believe that you receive them, and ye shall have them' (Mark 11:24).

THE PRAYER OF FAITH WILL GET GOD'S ATTENTION!

FACT 37

Prayer Of Faith Will Produce Wisdom When Needed

'If any lack wisdom, let him ask of God, that giveth to all men liberally, and upbraideth not; and it shall be given him. But let him ask in faith, nothing wavering. For he that wavereth is like a wave of the sea driven with the wind and tossed. For let not that man think he shall receive any thing of the Lord' (James 1:5-7).

PRAYER OF FAITH WILL PRODUCE WISDOM WHEN NEEDED!

FACT 38

Faith Will Be Tried

'That the trial of your faith...though it be tried with fire, might be found unto praise and honour and glory at the appearing of Jesus Christ:'

1 Peter 1:7

FAITH AN IMPORTANT SUBJECT TO MAN

'Knowing this, that the trying of your faith worketh patience.'

James 1:2

'Blessed is the man that endureth temptation: for when he is tried, he shall receive the crown of life, which the Lord hath promise to them that love him.'

James 1:12

Faith will be tried to prove its worth.
FAITH WILL BE TRIED!

FACT 39

Faith Will Be Made Impotent By Doubt, Unbelief And Fear

'And he said come. And when Peter was come down out of the ship, he walked on the water, to go to Jesus. But when he saw the wind boisterous, he was afraid; and beginning to sink, he cried, saying, Lord, save me. And immediately Jesus stretched forth his hand, and caught him, and said unto him, o thou of little faith, wherefore didst thou doubt?'

Matthew 14:29-31

'As soon as Jesus heard the word that was spoken, he saith unto the ruler of the Synagogue, be not afraid, only believe.'

Mark 5:36

'And Jesus answering saith unto them, have faith in God. For verily I say unto you, that whosoever shall say unto this mountain, be thou removed, and be thou cast into the sea; and shall not doubt in his heart, but shall believe that those things which he saith shall come to pass; he shall have whatsoever he saith. Therefore I say unto you, what things so ever ye desire, when you pray, believe that ye receive them, and ye shall have them.'

Mark 11:23-24

FAITH WILL BE MADE IMPOTENT BY DOUBT, UNBELIEF AND FEAR!

FACT 40

Faith Will Be Contend For

There will be a need to agonise, for the faith in God. The Bible says in Jude 3;

'Beloved, when I gave all diligence to write unto you of the common salvation, it was needful for me to write unto you, exhort you that ye should earnestly contend for the faith which was once delivered unto the saints.'

In 1 Timothy 6:11-14 Apostle Paul wrote to Timothy to:

'... follow after righteousness, godliness, faith, love, patience, and meekness. Fight the good fight of faith, lay hold on eternal life, whereunto thou art also called, and hast professed a good profession before many witnesses. I give thee charge in the sight of God, who quickeneth all things, and before Christ Jesus, who before Pontius Pilate witnessed a good confession; That thou keep this commandment without spot, unrebukeable, until the appearing of our Lord Jesus Christ.'

Apostle Paul wrote:

'I have fought a good fight, I have finished my course, I have kept the faith:'

FAITH WILL BE CONTEND, FOR!

FACT 41

Faith Will Be Spoken Of

'First, I thank my God through Jesus Christ for you all, that your faith is spoken of throughout the whole world.'

Romans 1:8

Jesus spoke of the faith of Peter when he walk on water and he later became afraid to the point that he started drowning in Matthew 14:31; *'And immediately Jesus stretched forth his hand, and caught him, and said unto him, O thou of little faith, wherefore didst thou doubt?'*

In Matthew 8:10; Jesus spoke of the centurion's faith. Saying; *'… verily I say unto you I have not found so great faith, no, not in Israel.'* Paul the Apostle in Romans 4:19-20; spoke of Abraham's faith, saying:

'And being not weak in faith, he considered not his own body now dead, when he was about an hundred years old, neither yet the deadness of Sarah's womb: He staggered not at the promise of God through unbelief; but was strong in faith giving glory to God;'

FAITH WILL BE SPOKEN OF!

FACT 42

Faith Will Be Built Up By Praying In The Will Of God

Faith can fluctuate from time to time, because

FAITH AN IMPORTANT SUBJECT TO MAN

man is in constant warfare with the adversary (devil). And in order to overcome, our faith must be in use constantly.

> 'And this is the victory that over cometh the world, even our faith.'
>
> 1 John 5:4

As a car battery requires a charger to keep the battery power fully charged (built-up) when in use, likewise is our faith needing to be kept built -up.

'Jude 20; says

> 'But ye, beloved, building up yourselves on your most holy faith, praying in the Holy Ghost.'

FAITH WILL BE BUILT UP BY PRAYING IN THE WILL OF GOD!

CHAPTER SEVEN

THE *SHOULD - BE* OF FAITH

The God kind of faith needs to be based on the right premise - in order to be divinely potent. This premise is what I called The Should — Be of Faith - which is as follows:

FACT 43

Faith Should Be Motivated By Love

'For we through the Spirit wait for the hope of righteousness by faith. for in Jesus Christ neither circumcision availeth anything, nor uncircumcision; but faith which worketh by love.'

Galatians 5:6

FAITH AN IMPORTANT SUBJECT TO MAN

Faith is not to be motivated by Greed, Selfishness, Covetousness or need; but faith is to be motivated, energised, and kept working by love which is released in our heart by the Holy Spirit.

> '... The love of God is shed abroad in our hearts by the Holy Ghost, which is given unto us.'
>
> **Romans 5:5**

FAITH SHOULD BE MOTIVATED BY LOVE!

CHAPTER EIGHT

MORE FACTS ABOUT FAITH

There is more facts about the God kind of faith - which will be worthy of mentioning in this chapter. These are as follows:

FACT 44

Not Everyman Has Faith

'And he said, I will hide my face from them, I will see what their end shall be: for they are a very froward generation, children in whom is no faith.'

Deuteronomy 32: 20

'... for all men have not Faith.'

2 Thessalonians 3:2

FAITH AN IMPORTANT SUBJECT TO MAN

The following are the consequences of lack of Faith:

1. In Galatians 3:10 *'For as many as are of the works of the law are under the curse: for it is written, Cursed is every one that continueth not in all things which are written in the book of the law to do them.'*

2. Job 9:2-3 *'I know it is so of a truth: but how should man be just with? If he will contend with him, he cannot answer him one of a thousand.'*

3. John 8: 51 *'Verily, verily, I say unto you, If a man keep my saying, he shall never see death.'*

4. Revelations 22: 14 *'Blessed are they that do his commandments, that they may have right to the tree of life, and may enter in through the gates into the city.'*

5. Luke 13: 6-9 *'He spake also this parable; A certain man had a fig tree planted in his vine yard; and he came and sought fruit thereon, and found none. Then said he unto the dresser of his vineyard, behold, these three years I come seeking fruit on this fig tree, and find none: cut it down; why cumbereth it the ground? And he answering said unto him, lord, let it alone this year also, till I shall dig about it, and dung it: And if it bear fruit, well: and if not, then after that thou shall cut it down."*

Faith only comes by hearing from God, not every man hears from God.

SO, NOT EVERY MAN HAS FAITH!

FACT 45

Faith Is Given, In The Same Measure To Every Man

When faith comes to a man, it comes in a measure. This measure however, can be developed by feeding on God's word and by deployment to make the faith stronger.

God gives the same measure of faith to every man, that faith comes to.

> '... but to think soberly, according as God hath dealt to every man the measure of faith.'
>
> **Romans 12:3**

(For further insight on developing your faith read my mini-book titled 'How to Develop Your Faith')

FAITH IS GIVEN TO EVERY MAN IN THE SAME MEASURE!

FAITH AN IMPORTANT SUBJECT TO MAN

FACT 46

Faith Goes Only Where Hope Is

'Now, faith is the substance of things hoped for,...' (Hebrew 11:1).

FAITH GOES ONLY TO WHERE HOPE IS!

CHAPTER NINE

THE ACCOMPLISH- MENTS OF FAITH

The God kind of faith has many accomplishments and here are some of them.

FACT 47

Faith Has Accomplished Much

Faith has accomplished much. By faith the elders in the faith obtained a good report.

> 'Now, faith is the substance of things hoped for, the evidence of things not seen. For by it the elders obtained a good report. Through faith we understand that the worlds were framed by God's Word, so that things which are seen were not made of things which do appear.
>
> By faith Abel offered unto God a more excellent sacrifice than Cain, by which he obtained witness that he was

FAITH AN IMPORTANT SUBJECT TO MAN

righteous, God testifying of his gifts: and by it he being dead yet speaketh.

By faith Enouch was translated that he should not see death; and was not found, because God had translated him: for before his translation he had this testimony, that he pleased God.

By faith Noah, being warned of God of things not seen as yet, moved with fear, prepared an ark to the saving of his house; by the which he condemned the world, and became heir of the righteousness which is by faith.

By faith Abraham, when he was called to go out into a place which he should after receive for an inheritance, obeyed; and he went out, not knowing whither he went. By faith he sojourned in the land of promise, as in a strange country, dwelling in tabernacles with Isaac and Jacob, the heirs with him of the same promise: For he looked for a city which hath foundations, whose builder and maker is God.

Through faith also Sarah herself received strength to conceive seed, and was delivered of a child when she was past age, because she judged him faithful who had promised. And so a whole nation came from Abraham, who was too old to have even one child - a nation with so many millions of people that, like stars of the sky and the sand on the ocean shores, there is no way to count them.

Living Bible Edition

By faith Abraham, when he was tired, offered up Isaac; and he that had received the promises offered up his only begotten son, of whom it was said, That in Isaac shall thy seed be called: He believed that if Isaac died God would bring him back to life again; and that is just about what happened, for as far as Abraham was concerned, Isaac was doomed to death, but he came back again alive.

Living Bible Edition

By faith Isaac blessed Jacob and Esau concerning things to come.

By faith Jacob, when he was a dying, blessed both the sons of Joseph; and worshipped, leaning upon the top of his staff.

By faith Joseph, when he died, made mention of the departing of the children of Israel; and gave commandment concerning his bones.

By faith Moses, when he was born, was hid three months of his parents, because they saw he was a proper child; and they were not afraid of the king's commandment.

By faith Moses, when he was come to years, refused to be called the son of Pharaoh's daughter; choosing rather to suffer affliction with the people of God, than to enjoy the pleasure of sin for a season; Esteeming the reproach of Christ greater riches than the treasure in Egypt: for he had respect unto the recompense of the reward.

By faith he forsook Egypt, not fearing the wrath of the king: for he endured, as seeing him who is invisible. Through faith he kept the Passover, and the sprinkling of blood, lest he that destroyed the firstborn should touch them.

By faith they passed through the Red sea as by dry land: which the Egyptians assaying to do were drowned.

By faith the walls of Jericho fell down, after they were compassed about seven days.

FAITH AN IMPORTANT SUBJECT TO MAN

By faith the harlot Rahab perished not with them that believed not, when she had received the spies with peace.

And what shall I more say? For the time would fail me to tell of Gideon, and of Barak, and of Samson, and of Jephthan; of David also, and Samuel, and of the Prophets: who through faith subdued kingdoms, wrought righteousness, obtained promises, stopped the mouths of lions, Quenched the violence of fire, escaped the edge of the sword, out of weakness were made strong, waxed valiant in fight, turned to flight the armies of the aliens.

Women received their dead raised to life again: and others were tortured, not accepting deliverance; that they might obtain a better resurrection: And others had trial of cruel mockings and scourgings, yea, more over of bonds and imprisonment: They were stoned, they were sawn asunder, were tempted, were slain with the sword: they wondered in deserts, and in mountains, and in dens and caves of the earth.

And these all, having obtained a good report through faith, ...'

Hebrews 11:1-5, 7-39

FAITH HAS ACCOMPLISHED MUCH!

DECISION!

Will you accept Jesus as your Lord and Saviour today? The Bible says,

'For whosoever shall call upon the name of the Lord shall be saved.'

Romans 10:13

'That if thou shall confess with thy mouth the Lord Jesus, and shall believe in thine heart that God hath raised him from the dead, thou shall be saved. For with the heart man believeth unto righteousness; and with the mouth, confession is made unto salvation.

Romans 10:9-10

To receive Jesus Christ as Lord and Saviour of your life, please pray this prayer from your heart now!

"Dear Jesus, thank you for dying for me on the Cross, and for my deliverance from sin and its consequences. I acknowledged that I am a sinner and I ask you, for forgiveness. I confess you now, as my Lord and saviour. Thank you for my Salvation, the gift of the Holy Spirit and faith in you. Amen."

FAITH AN IMPORTANT SUBJECT TO MAN

☐ YES! Brother Akin Akintola, I made a decision to accept Christ as my Lord and Saviour today.

☐ Please send me a free copy of your mini-book **'Now that I've said YES TO JESUS! WHAT'S NEXT?'**

Name._____

Address _____

Postcode _____

Email _____

MAIL TO:
REV'D AKIN AKINTOLA
P.O. BOX 802,
CROYDON CRO9 8BB
UNITED KINGDOM.

OR EMAIL:
revakintola@hotmail.com

HELP US SPREAD THE GOOD NEWS! BE A PART OF GLOBAL EVANGELISM AND REVIVAL!!

When you link up with this Ministry in covenant partnership, you are directly influencing people you may never meet in your lifetime.

Your faithful prayers and finances help us to reach out to people all over the world with the gospel of Jesus Christ through Conferences, Conventions, Church meetings, Schools, Audio and video tapes, Printed materials, Radio and Television.

As a Covenant partner, every person that hears the good news through this ministry has you to thank.

Each one, who is saved, touched, healed or delivered by the Lord, has you to thank. You can be a vital part of Global Evangelism, Revival and the Great Harvest of Souls.

(You can be a New "Covenant Partner" by making a commitment to financially support this Ministry on a Regular basis.)

FAITH AN IMPORTANT SUBJECT TO MAN

☐ Yes, I would like to become a Covenant Partner to Gospel Faith Ministries International.

☐ Enclosed is my first gift of: $/£ ._____

I am sowing a one-time gift offering to this Ministry of: $/£ _____

Name._____

Address _____

Postcode _____

Email _____

Please Send to Our Address Nearest To You:
Gospel Faith Ministries International

In The United Kingdom

P.O Box 802, Croydon CR9 8BB
United Kingdom.

In The USA

P.O Box 1478
Washington DC 20013
USA.

OR EMAIL:
revakintola@hotmail.com

Gospel Faith Ministries International UK. Regd Charity No. 1056619

Audio & video tape offers from GFMI that will change your life forever!

This two tape series will keep you focused on God's purpose for your life.

This four tape series gives nuggets that will help you to lunch a powerful prayer life

Discover what the prayer of faith is and how it is prayed in this two tape series.

Believers are to pray without ceasing... learn the art of effective praying through this eight tape series.

This four tape series will get you connected to the anointing to trouble your troubles.

This two tape series takes you - to understand the reasons for the delay in receiving answers to your prayers.

Discover what this hindrances can be and how to roll them away in this two tape series.

In this four tape series you will know when God speaks, how He speaks and how to discern your God given purpose.

This five tape series takes you to having an understanding of the spiritual war

Discover how to study God's Word for great profits through this video.

ORDER FORM

CODE	DESCRIPTION	UNIT COST	PRICE
AAM0001	Why The Delay? (2 tapes)-	£8.00	
AAM0002	Discerning God's Purpose For Your Life (4 Tapes)	£16.00	
AAM0003	Call To War (5 Tapes)	£20.00	
AAM0004	16 Nuggets To A Successful Prayer Life (4 Tapes)	£16.00	
AAM0005	Victorious Christian Living (4 Tapes)	£16.00	
AAM0006	The Prayer of Faith (2 Tapes)	£8.00	
AAM0007	Rolling Away The Hindrances (2 Tapes)	£8.00	
AAM0008	Plugging Into God's purpose Through Prayer (2 Tapes)	£8.00	
AAM0009	The Effectual Prayer (8 Tapes)	£32.00	
AAM00010	Studying The Word For Maximum Effectiveness (video)	£10.00	
POSTAGE & PACKAGING UK Orders – Please add 5% of order Outside The UK – Please add 10% of order		**Total Enclosed**	

FAITH AN IMPORTANT SUBJECT TO MAN

Your Prayer Request Is Very Important To Me!

You are very important to God- that He is keeping a watch over His promises concerning you to make sure is fulfilled. Write and let me know when that devil raises its ugly head or you have a spiritual need. I will agree with you in prayer and also write back to you the counsel of the Lord that will help you receive the answer to your need. For the bible says in Matthew 18:19

"..., That if two of you shall agree on earth as touching any thing that they shall ask, it shall be done for them of my father which is in heaven."

(Please Print and use a separate sheet if necessary)

_____
_____
_____

Name._____

Address _____

Postcode _____

Email _____